D0891351

SEE BOB RUN &
WILD ABANDON

See Bob Run &
Wild Abandon

Daniel MacIvor

Playwrights Canada Press
Toronto

PLAYWRIGHTS CANADA PRESS
269 Richmond St. W., Suite 202, Toronto, ON M5V 1X1
416.703.0013 • info@playwrightscanada.com • www.playwrightscanada.com

For professional or amateur production rights, please contact:
Pam Winter at the Gary Goddard Agency
10 St. Mary's Street, Suite 800, Toronto, ON M4Y 1P9
416.928.0299, goddard@canadafilm.com

We acknowledge the financial support of the Canada Council for the Arts, the Ontario
Arts Council, the Ontario Media Development Corporation, and the Government of
Canada through the Canada Book Fund for our publishing activities.

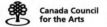 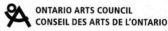

Cover photo of Daniel MacIvor by Keith Penner
Book design by Blake Sproule

LIBRARY AND ARCHIVES CANADA CATALOGUING IN PUBLICATION
MacIvor, Daniel, 1962-
    See Bob run ; &, Wild abandon / Daniel MacIvor. -- 2nd ed.

Plays.
Issued also in electronic formats.
ISBN 978-0-88754-997-7

    I. Title. II. Title: Wild abandon.

PS8575.I86S4 2011   C812'.54   C2011-904309-2

First edition: March 1990
Second revised edition: February 2013
Printed and bound in Canada by Imprimerie Gauvin, Gatineau

The Heart of the Actor

When I wrote first wrote *See Bob Run* I never considered that
I would, twenty-five years later while performing in a play of
mine at the Stratford Festival, be writing a new foreword to the
play's re-publication. I don't know that I really considered much
of anything about the future at that time. I wasn't considering my
career or my body of work or anything else, I was concerned about
telling a story—and writing a play that would convince my best
friend to move to Toronto from Halifax to perform it—that was
it. *See Bob Run* was written quickly, without workshops, without
extensive dramaturgy, without asking too many questions about
why. Of course, perhaps this has to do with the foolish genius of
youth. These days I could not write a play in that way—I couldn't
imagine working without a dramaturge, without a clear sense
of my audience, and I would be too bogged down with the why
questions and concerns about how the play would reflect my body
of work, my "career."

Wild Abandon came a year later, and even here one can see that I was starting to think about things beyond storytelling. I was already asking questions about the why of storytelling, and because of that *Wild Abandon* is a more difficult play to access than *See Bob Run*. And while the *See Bob Run* you hold is the original, there are actually two versions of *Wild Abandon*—a shorter version that was performed in a solo-performance festival in Toronto and this version, extended into a longer play. The first version is long lost, written ages before the days of hard drives and the eternal life of the Digital Universe. So clearly with this *Wild Abandon* I had begun a relationship with dramaturgy, and with the success of *See Bob Run* I had started to catch the whiff of a career and all the odd concerns such thoughts bring. But even still, beyond my simple thoughts about non-linear and open-to-interpretation narrative, *Wild Abandon* came from a clear and direct desire to put myself on stage in my own work and to expose the heart of the actor.

Of all the plays I have written, *See Bob Run* and *Wild Abandon* have probably had the most impact—the plays found their way into high schools and are done often there, and based on conversations I have had with artistic directors across the country, monologues from both these plays are by far the most seen in general auditions—some ADs can actually recite parts of Steve's diner speech from *Wild Abandon* based on how many times they have seen young actors perform it. And when I ask myself why, I am drawn to consider who Bob and Steve are, who they represent. Both are outsiders; from the outset neither seem to fit the mould of who everyone else appears to be—both misunderstood, both feeling unloved, both so lonely. This loneliness seems to me the key to why any of us do the things we do. Most of us spend our lives doing anything—marrying for the sake of marrying, immersing ourselves in our careers, numbing ourselves with television and alcohol, losing ourselves in dreams of what might be—rather than just sitting in the "is" of our lives. Because in that "is" exists a kind of loneliness. But what I understand now at the age of fifty, and what neither Bob nor Steve can quite come to grips with—certainly not at the beginning of their stories—is that that's okay. The Buddhists say that the perfect way to view life is through tears, tears brought on by the beauty of all things and the knowledge that all this beauty is temporary. And in that is a kind of loneliness, but we can take great solace in the fact that we are all alone together. And that, I think, is what the heart of the actor understands. We come to this work with our wounds exposed. Our loneliness, our outsider nature, our knowledge that time is a joke and the joke is on us, our longing for connection. In each of us is a Bob or a Steve or some combination of the two. To play either Bob or Steve is not to take a trip outside the self to embody some invented character, but rather to take our own actor hearts in our hands and fearfully offer them to a room full of strangers, asking for love while saying we don't want it, wanting their acceptance while pretending it doesn't mater.

Do as you will with these plays, find your own way through, but from my perspective I can tell you that by the end of each play, with Bob on her beach and with Steve counting on past three to four, each have discovered their place in this lonely, temporary, beautiful world. Each have found their heart in the dark room of strangers. Enjoy the view, and dance.

—Daniel MacIvor
Stratford, Ontario
August 2012

See Bob Run

For Caroline

See Bob Run was first produced by Buddies In Bad Times Theatre and da da kamera in 1987 at the Poor Alex Theatre, Toronto.

BOB   Caroline Gillis

Directed by Ken McDougall
Designed by Steve Mici Lucas
Stage managed by Claudine Domingue
Original music by Ron-Doug Parks

The Set

There should be no effort to create a "real" highway, a "real" car. It is as if Bob has rented the space and built the set to tell her story to this audience tonight.

In the Toronto production the set was a single bucket seat, a section of chain-link fence stage left, a section of picket fence stage right. A dotted line ran up the centre aisle of the theatre.

*The set: the Trans-Canada Highway. In the middle of the road
is a single car seat on a platform. On one side a weather-beaten
picket fence, on the other a rusted chain-link fence. The fences
and highway bend off into exaggerated perspective upstage.*

*Darkness. We hear "Brought a Love." It fades. The sound of a car
approaching. Headlights move across the stage. In the headlights we see a young woman sitting in the car seat. Darkness.
Another car. Darkness. Another car. This time when* BOB *is seen
in the headlights they freeze on her. They become bright. She
steps out of the seat.*

BOB

Once upon a time there was a king and a queen. And they were
married. The king was handsome and strong and everybody thought
he was good 'cause he was, most of the time, and he was good
even to the queen who was a witch. She was ugly and mean and
a witch who put spells on people 'cause she hated everybody.
That's how she got the king to marry her, by putting a spell on
him so he'd think she was pretty good and that. But she wasn't.
Aaaaaaand... all the king wanted was a princess. He wanted a

7

princess so bad. A little princess that he could put on his knee and give big wet kisses to. And the queen says "No." "No way," she says. She doesn't want a princess 'cause she knows what'll happen. She knows that the king will end up lovin the princess so much that he won't love her anymore—even though he hardly does now anyway. That's when the king starts to get mad. He wants a princess. It's all he wants. And because she won't give it to him he gets full of hate. Full of hate for her. And they start fightin all the time. One night it gets real bad and they both lose their voices from yelling about the princess. And then. The king grabs the queen and throws her down and makes her make sex right there on the floor in the kitchen. The cold, cold kitchen floor. They're doin it but they're not thinkin about love, they're thinkin about hate. He's thinkin about how he's stabbin her with his thing and she's thinkin about how she wishes she could close herself up so tight she would cut it right off him. And it's over. And they're layin there on the floor in the kitchen starin at the ceilin and the king reaches over and puts his hand on the queen's belly and he knows. He knows. She's pregnant. And she was it turns out. That's what the doctor says. And the king is so happy he's jumpin up and down and singin. The queen has never seen him like this before. And she gets even worse. More ugly, more stupid, more hateful. 'Cause she knows. The king is gonna love the princess more than her. So she puts a spell on herself. She's a witch so she can do that. And months and months go by and she's gettin bigger and bigger. Lookin pregnant and that. Then, this night, she starts gettin pains that the baby's comin, so the king runs and gets the doctor. The doctor comes and goes in the queen's room. The king's waitin outside the door. He's waitin forever. Then, the part comes where the baby's supposed to cry but the king don't hear nothin. Another long time goes by and the king's freakin out that somethin's wrong. Then he hears this sound. This long loud ugly sound. And this gross smell. He doesn't know what's goin on. Then finally out comes the doctor and he's got this look on his face and the king says "What?" and the doctor looks at the king and says... "The queen wasn't pregnant at all; she was just full of shit."

BOB laughs.

The end.

It is night in a car. BOB speaks to the driver.

Bob.
Roberta.
Bob.
East. I'm headed east. Until you hit water. A lot of water.

You don't got a radio in here?
Man that's pretty weird.

Only reason to have a car. Radio on wheels. Roll up the windows and you got your own studio. Right? Drivin along bein in any band you want. Man, I'd have one. And speakers like this... huge. Make a wind. I always got a radio. I even got one in my bag but it needs electricity. I hate no music. You gotta have music man, it's the best. I like all kinds too. Every kind. Don't matter what as long as it's music. 'Cept for that stuff they play in offices and that so you don't even notice it. That's not music, that's just bad air. Pollution right. But every other kind I like. Even, like, Johnny Cash? You know. People think he's dumb but he's really not. He always wears black 'cause the world's so bad right. That's pretty neat. All kinds. You don't like it eh? Some people say it's just noise, but that's 'cause they're not really listenin. Once you listen to it, once you really listen to it... that's it, you're gone. Like me man. I'd die if I didn't have it eh. Makes me talk when I don't have music and I don't like talkin.

I don't usually talk this much... some people pick you up 'cause they need somebody to talk to drivin eh. Them are the people who don't have radios.

Talkin talkin words words... all them words and nothin gets said. That's why music's the best right. There's words but then there's music to really make them mean somethin. Like, you know what I mean?

Like, you can say: "Bob got a gun." Or, you can sing: (singing) "Bob got a gun, oooo, Bob got a gun gun gun... " See. Singin makes it mean more.

BOB *laughs.*

Just kiddin buddy.

Just kiddin.

Black. Night in another car.

Bob.

Roberta.

Bob.

Nobody ever called me Roberta. Ever. Even when I was just a baby. I think they only wrote "Roberta" on the papers 'cause the doctors or priest or whoever wouldn't let them put "Bob." No middle name either. Just Bob. My mother wouldn't let them give me a middle name. "One name's enough," she said. Easy to say and remember. And spell. Just three little letters. Two the same. I think it's okay though. Not like some dumb names. Like Jennifer. What's a Jennifer? Or Linda. What's a Linda? Even like, my best friend is Tamara, which sounds nice but it's pretty dumb anyway right? Like, she herself says it's dumb. Which it is. If you're gonna call somebody somethin you should call them somethin that they're like. I don't know if I'm like a Bob though. People say it's a good name for me. Better than Roberta. This girl when I was in school, Roberta Robina Bonaparte, she was fat and had glasses. Her mother made her wear ugly clothes and take tap-dancin lessons... Man I don't think dancin's supposed to be noisy. Every time we had a show at school Roberta'd do this bad tap dancin to that song "Knock Three Times" by Tony

Orlando and Dawn. Which was a dumb song even then. She was a perfect Roberta. You know?

If I had a kid, and I doubt it, but if I did I'd name it Shiny.
Shiny.
'Cause that's what I'd want it to be.

Do radios cost extra in cars or what?

Black. Gentle light up slowly. A car. BOB *is sleeping.*

Timmy...

The car stops suddenly and BOB *is jerked awake.*

Jesus! What?... Oh shit man... No that's okay that's okay.
Shit. I was sleepin... I was... I was havin a dream about... where are we?
Timmy? What about Timmy? Yeah? What I say?
Just Timmy?
That's my ex-boyfriend. What I say? Nothin—just "Timmy"?
Why was I sayin that I wonder.
I wasn't dreamin about him. I was dreamin about... this great dream... standin in the water right up to my neck... and there's that big weird animal... Timmy wasn't there though. He wasn't anywhere. He's my ex-boyfriend. But I don't know if he knows he's my ex-boyfriend or not. I suppose he does eh.

'Cause I'm here and he's there. Too bad some ways. We had a band right? Finger Prince. It was his band really. He was Timmy Prince. It was his band but he let me join up. And not just 'cause I was his girlfriend either. It was 'cause I sing great backup and I'm a wicked dancer. That's what he said. It was so good at first. Before he got fucked.

Excuse my language.

You never heard a song until you heard Timmy Prince sing it. That's what everybody used to say. He could clean the air with his singin. Like it wasn't a pretty voice but it was really real. Right from his heart. People would shut right up and listen. Even drunk. It was somethin. Best band I ever heard 'cause of Timmy. Tamara said he was gonna be a star eh? A big one. He thought I was good too. At the end before the band split up he even had me singin lead on a song. "Baby Tonight." Dylan right? I'd sing lead he'd sing backup. It was excellent. We put it right at the end of the last set. There'd be people cryin.

Too bad what happened but it had to.
I don't wanna talk about that.

You ever play that game?
When you were a kid?
"Who Falls Dead the Best"? We played it up in the graveyard. One person starts as the gunner and everybody else took turns runnin by and gettin shot and whoever falls dead the best gets to be gunner.

We played it on this big triangle of grass… in the graveyard. There'd be like fifteen of us playin. Everybody doin all this fancy dyin, flyin through the air or rollin down the hill or doin spins. Most people died like it was a kinda dance. We played all the time. It was our game.

Weird eh?

It's not really like that you know.

Black. Lights up. BOB is standing at the side of the road waiting for a ride.

No cars. She waits. She begins to sing softly to herself and slowly realizes she is alone and liking the sound of her voice on the empty highway. She increases her volume. She gets very loud. A dog begins to bark. Another. Every dog within five miles.

Shit.

Black. BOB in a spot.

There was this big weird animal in the closet. This big weird animal. And it was in the closet. The little girl who was born a princess and a pile of shit is always scared when she goes to bed at night because she knows it's there. She can see it peakin out and she can hear it breathin. It's real for sure. But no one else believes her and call her dreamin when she talks about it. A bad dream. And she says, "But there is an animal in the closet, I can hear it breathin!" And her mother says, "Shut up. Grow up. Bad dream." And after a while she starts thinkin maybe it is a dream. And just when she starts believin that, that's when the door of the closet opens and there it is. This big weird naked animal. And it's smilin. But not friendly. Or too friendly so it's scary. And it comes over to her in her bed where she's starin at it and it says: "Hold on to my handle, do that. See it, there's my happy handle. Come on. Hold it and make me happy." So she does and it makes it happy. And the big weird animal is so happy it never goes back into the closet again. It's always waitin for her. But it's okay for the little girl now. Now she knows, it's just a dream.

Black. Night in another car.

Bob.
Just Bob.
'Cause it's just Bob that's all.
You got a cigarette?
Too bad.
Yeah cancer. Bad stuff.

Cancer's really weird eh? Like you can look smooth and clean on the outside but inside you're all rotten and black... Like bad people. Like my mother. She's really ugly and mean inside but if you were standin behind her in line at the grocery store she'd let you get in front of her if you had less stuff or if you came to the door sellin a chocolate bar for kids with no legs she'd buy one or even maybe two... she tricks everybody. Makes them think she's good. But she's not. My father told me how she really was. See, she even had me tricked for a while 'cause I remember once I got this flu and she comes into the living room where I'm sleepin and she sits by me and puts my head on her lap, my face is pressin right up against her good skirt makin it all wet with my sweat but she don't care and she was doin this to my hair... See, she was trickin me. She can't be good 'cause... she can't be good 'cause she kicked my father out for nothing. I come home from school one day and Children's Aid is there and she's pretendin to be cryin and she says to me, in front of them right, she says, "It's okay baby, he's gone, he won't come back and he won't be able to hurt you anymore." He never hurt me... never... just loved me more that's all... just loved me more...

Pause.

She's livin with this guy now who smells so bad.

Pause.

You ever kill anybody?

Black. BOB *is standing left of the car seat. The seat is not visible.*

Tamara and me would get all dressed up to go out. She had the greatest stuff. Leopard-skin jumpsuit she always let me wear. And she had these wicked, wicked boots. Fringes on 'em. She'd be walkin in 'em and it'd be like there was waves movin around her ankles. So we'd get all dressed up. Lookin really hot with the perfect earrings. And then we'd take a taxi down the Corral. Get there about ten, ten thirty, dependin on the band, and walk in at the break. The guys would look at us and be droolin and the girls would look at us like sluts or lovin Tamara's boots or whatever. At the bar we'd each order a zombie and two beers. By the time the band started playin again we'd be ready to have a good time. Yeah! Dancin! So wild. The band would be lovin us 'cause we were part of it and makin everybody dance. After a while they'd start playin everything right to us, especially the slow ones. Like "Angie" and Spyder's song about "Love Me Now" or whatever. I'd get off so bad. It was perfect 'cause I was imaginin that it was me they were singin about or that I was in the band doin backup. Tamara though, she liked it 'cause she could see which guy she wanted or which guy wanted her. She had a way to do it. First the lead singer, then the bass player, then the other guys, and always the drummer last. She said to save the best for last. Mostly all I wanted was to be in the band... Tamara wanted the band to be in her. Yeah, yeah that's it eh. I wanted to be in the band and Tamara wanted the band to be in her.

Then there's this night I will never forget. Everything goes the same except we're goin to see Finger Prince which I never seen but Tamara did one time at Backstreet. She says, "You gotta see em, Bob." So I figure she thinks she can get one of em. But she was right man. I had to see em. I had to see Timmy Prince. Man he was somethin. He was the world. And it was when he was singin, even when he was singin his own songs, that he was the most beautiful thing I ever before saw. He was more than a person. I'm so flipped out I never even had a sip of the zombie. Freakin. Like I gotta meet him after the last set. Tamara gets us back to the change room. I'm standin there in front of him not sayin nothing like I was retarded or somethin. After a while he looks up at me and smiles and says, "Hello princess."

Black. Night in another car.

Nice car for a girl.

You make a lot of money?

I wish.

Maybe I'll get somethin where I'm goin.

East.

To the water.

Pause.

Jeeze... Bob.

Yeah! Roberta yeah!

That's pretty neat, nobody ever gets that.

Yeah I think it's good too.

Just Bob though.

Nobody ever calls me Roberta.

No. I useta have a boyfriend but not anymore. Not since three o'clock. And I'm not gonna have another one for a long time either. Maybe never. No way. It's too dumb and fake. And it gives me a headache. You know? Yeah, girls are better. You should meet my best friend Tamara. Man, she's got it right. She doesn't let no guy take her no place she don't wanna go. She's got balls this big. I shoulda told her I was leavin but I didn't have time, you know. Maybe I'll write her a letter though once I get where I'm goin. Maybe she'll come down or something.

What?

What? What do ya mean?

I don't... Hey, I don't do that okay.

I don't do that okay.

I'll get out right up here.

I'm not scared.

This is far enough.

Stop. Stop the fuckin car lady!

    BOB gets out of the car.

Jesus.

Nobody's safe from nobody no more or fuckin what.

BOB crosses the stage.

I told my mother to get fucked and I left.

I even said that to her.

"GET FUCKED WOMAN!"

And I left and I went to stay at Tamara's place.

Sometimes I stayed in Tamara's bed with her 'cause it was a big bed and there was nothing wrong with that. And sometimes I would let her hold me 'cause she was lonely and she'd be cryin. Everybody gets lonely. Like I even wore her clothes. It was like we were sisters. I would like it when she held me. She was so soft. It wasn't sick though. If I was sad it would make me feel better too. It wasn't sick. It was just two sisters who were sad.

And that's where I was stayin when I met Timmy.

Tamara hated Timmy.

Maybe she was jealous but there's nothin wrong with that.

We were the best friends in the world.

She'd be happy now though I bet eh.

Timmy said she was a weirdo. She isn't a weirdo. Well.

Maybe she is but if she is it's in a good way. The first night I met her she was so great. Like I'm at a party at Leo's place and I was drinkin hard liquor and smoking somethin. Stupid. 'Cause now I know I can't do that without freakin out. Man that night I was so flipped. I'm sittin on the steps at Leo's and I think I'm dyin. Then Tamara who I never even met before comes out and sits on the steps way over on the other side. Starin at me outta the corner of her eyes. Then she says to me, really serious: "You're not gonna stab me or anything are you?" And I say "No." And she says, "Good 'cause everybody in there is." And we're real quiet. Then she starts laughin, at herself. Then I start laughin 'cause she was freaked out the same way I was, and just because she laughed so funny. She laughs like this like hardly any sound comes out but her whole body's shakin and her face is froze up like this...

She laughs so funny.

Then, all of a sudden she jumps off the steps and starts dancin. Like there's no music but she grabs me and gets me to dance too. Then she says, "Come on!" and we go dancin up the middle of the street to the Donut Castle. We get inside and some dumb station is on the radio, like Engelbert Humperdink, but we're still dancin.

Everybody's lookin at us like we're nuts. And I like that you know? Sort of like we knew something they didn't.

We had this secret.

We order like six apple crullers and six Bavarian creams. Sat in the window and laughed and pigged out for about an hour. And that's even before I knew her name.

Then we're best friends. She says I can stay at her place to get away from my mother. And she gets me a job at the beauty parlour 'cause I didn't have one and I think we spent every single minute together. Every single minute for four months up until the second night of Finger Prince.

The second night of Finger Prince I went back to the Corral by myself. I sat right at the front of the stage 'cause I wanted to make sure Timmy Prince seen that I was there. He seemed so big and like he wasn't a person. He was like a song and from where he was standin he could reach down and pick me up in his hands. He could hold me way up above the ground where nobody could get me and there'd be this music...

After the last song he comes over to me and wants to drive me home. I say no I like walkin.

He leaves his car at the Corral and walks me.

We walk through the park and he tells me how the moon is really no light at all, just gets it from the sun. And how lilacs are the best flower 'cause nobody ever has to plant them and they just grow every year. All by themselves. 'Cause they want to. And that I should have a lake named after me. Lake Bob. And how he wishes he could bring me one.

All this perfect pretend.

And that's what was good see.

For a while.

Everything was like walkin through the park and pretendin. He never tried nothin. I never thought of it. I just wondered why he was wantin to talk to me all the time.

Tamara nearly had a fit this one time he comes to work to see me. Had a fit. She said 'cause we were busy. I say 'cause he brought me lilacs and a card with the moon on it.

And then nothin happened for a long time.

And then. That night on Tamara's sofa.

So quiet. Shh!

I don't remember it. I don't remember any of it.

Just after and how he looked like he was just a person... real... Like it wasn't Timmy Prince holdin me so quiet and dressin slow and leavin backwards out Tamara's front door. Just some person... some guy. Like the ones in school and the ones on the street.

After and me thinkin of how I was feelin this way I never felt before and the start of gettin sick.

After he goes home I took this bath so hot that next day it was like I had a sunburn.

And he wants me to move in and I say no.

And he wants me to move in and I say no.

And he wants me to move in and he brings me this bottle of pink water.

I say, "What is it?" He says: "It's your Lake Bob."

And I say yes I'll move in. 'Cause that wasn't real—see it was pretend and maybe he would be able to pretend forever.

But no.

And he's so gentle and soft, and every time it happens the sick gets worse. 'Cause it's all a lie see. That part's just for him.

It's supposed to hurt. But he kept wantin me to feel good in it.

That's not how it's supposed to be. All that gentle. It's a lie. When it's real it's a lie.

Only pretend it's true.

I know that. Now I know.

It's all about... I know see... It's all about when I was little...
a little kid. I know that now. I'm asleep. Or almost asleep. And he
comes into my room. But I don't open my eyes. And he's scared
you can tell. He is. He sits down at the edge of the bed. For this
long time. And after a while...

He... pulls... down... the... blanket... and... lifts... up...
my... shirt... and... rubs... his... hand... on... my... belly...
and... says...

Shhh.

Shhh. I'm not supposed to tell anybody. 'Cause Mommy's so
mean to him. And that it might hurt. And it does hurt... but that
isn't the important part. Don't think about the hurt.

Shhh.

Think about the water. All this water over you and the sound
of the waves. The important part is that I am his princess.

And I am his princess... and he loves me more than... more
than... more than anything anyone even the smartest man in the
world can think of... and... Daddy!

Shhh.

We'll just cuddle. Shhh we'll cuddle. I'll hold you and hold
you my little princess. Beautiful, beautiful, shhh...

And I will never go away and I will always always no matter
what be your daddy.

And he went away and never said nothing not even goodbye.
And I know he's at the water.

Isn't he?

Black. BOB *is leaning into a car.*

Are you married?
I said are you married?
Good.

BOB *gets in.*

This is your husband's car?
Oh yeah? Must be nice.
East.
Uh… Jennifer…
I'm goin east to meet my father.

Your husband give you this car?
It's nice.
I don't even know how to drive.

You love him eh?
Your husband.
Good. That's good. It's good you love somebody.
Nobody can stop you.

I'm just gonna go to sleep now okay.
That okay?

You ever been to the water?

It's nice eh?

I bet it is.

I can't wait to be there.

I'm just going to walk in up to my neck first thing.

Right up to my neck and just stand there.

Imagine what that would be like eh?

Lights fade. Bright headlights from the first scene.

So there's this dance. This big huge dance where you have to go with someone and wear flowers. Everybody's supposed to ask someone special to go with them. All the people from all around are going. They're going to have this special kind of romantic music and millions of Kleenex decorations. The little girl who is a princess and a pile of shit is going. She asks the big weird animal to go with her. Not 'cause she's scared but 'cause she wants him to. See it's just that he's weird not that he's mean. And he loves her so much. Really really. More than anything. The big weird animal says yes and he's so happy because he would love to go to the dance with the little girl. And it's exciting 'cause it's so special. They go. They get there. They walk in. Everybody stops. Everybody stops talkin and dancin and havin fun. All the nice romantic music stops. They are starin at the big weird animal and the little girl. Some people start pointin and laughin, some of them leave and some of them are so scared they get angry and say "Who let that thing in here?!" And it's just 'cause they're stupid or 'cause they don't understand that it's the most beautiful and perfect thing... the big weird animal and the little girl.

Nobody understands. And there's this witch there and she... No. The witch isn't there. But everybody's standin around laughin and yellin and that makes the big weird animal start to cry 'cause he's not mean at all and he's got the biggest, softest heart. So the little girl says, "Don't cry okay, don't cry, you're not bad, don't cry." And she takes him by the hand and she starts dancin with him in the middle of all these people, all around them, real quiet. They're dancin so slow and romantic and exquisite. The music starts again and it's perfect and the big weird animal stops cryin and starts smilin and they're the most excellent dancers. The most excellent dancers and other people start dancin again and other people until everybody's dancin again and everybody understands now and it's okay 'cause it's so good and all the people have the best time of their lives and the big weird animal and the little girl get the award for best dancers and the dance goes on and on and on ...

That whole last part isn't true.

The light shifts suddenly. BOB *steps downstage.*

I bet you could go downtown I bet in the middle of the day and stand on the corner and start screamin your head off—just screamin and makin noise and not stop—and they'd call some cops that'd take you away to some hospital where they'd stick a needle in your arm and then put you on some freak floor poppin a different colour pill in your mouth every ten minutes and I bet nobody'd even ask you "What's wrong?"

> BOB *opens her mouth to scream. A siren. Black. Lights up in the car.*

Shit man what's that? What they want? What's goin on? What were you doin? Were you speedin or something?

Why were you doin that, what were you doin?

Jesus I hate cops man. Well pull over or something!

The siren passes.

Oh man. It looked like they were after us though eh?

Didn't it?

Shit I was freakin.

Probably on their way to arrest some old lady for jaywalkin. Man they give me the creeps so bad. Like they can just walk up to you and arrest you or hit you or something just 'cause they don't like the way you look. That's scary eh? It's not even the guns though. It's the sticks. Those sticks. Oh man. The guns don't bug me. Daddy always had guns. Even taught me how to use 'em. They're not scary at all, 'cept if they don't work when you want 'em to. But the sticks. I never had any trouble with the cops.

Timmy though. Shit. He was always gettin arrested for somethin. Just 'cause what he looked like. 'Cause he wasn't bad or anything you know. He wasn't mean really. It was a different kind of mean. Know what I'm talkin about? You know what I'm talkin about? That's what drives me crazy that nobody does.

    BOB stands and steps forward.

Nobody knows what I'm talkin about.
Tamara said she did sort of.
I don't know if really.
See, when he was singin he was, he was... not real. And when he was talkin about lilacs and lakes and moons he was... not real. Sometimes it was so pretend it was perfect. Then he writes me this song. I didn't want him to, I said don't sing it but he did. It made me out to be something... special... and I'm not... see... I'm not special... at all. This song was "Brought a Love"... *(singing)* "I brought a love, in a cage, to your house, darling, and I let it go... " Him lookin at me and singin... It would make me feel real sick... throw-up kinda sick. And he'd get me on the bed. His mouth over my mouth and my eyes and my face and I couldn't breathe and he was suffocatin me, it was like, and I'd be starin at a picture or the ceiling, it's all hot and wet and he presses into me so I can't move and he's sayin "I love you I love you I love you" in this low voice all heavy and "It feels so good, don't it feel good"... and NO it didn't... this the bad part... this is the part where you're supposed to pretend... and these feelings... and

I'm scared I'm gonna get sick all over the place... one time I almost was... but I got up and run out the back door and over the fence and all the way past the store. To I don't even know where just runnin. Legs goin so far apart it's like I'm gonna split in two. And I only stopped 'cause my head hurt and I fell down. Maybe I never would've stopped. Maybe I would've run right to the water. That's where I was goin I bet. I never been there you know... when I was a princess... and in my room... and it was so dark... Daddy useta say... Shhh... "Think about the water"... the water knows everything... it knows everybody's biggest secrets... and it turns them into the sound of the waves at night and then it's okay 'cause everybody loves the sound of the waves at night. The water whisperin everybody's biggest secrets to you and you dream them nice. No bad dreams no scary dreams only nice dreams from it. And he promised me that some day...

Some day princess I'll take you to the water and you'll see and you'll hear...

And... I gave him my special and he took it with him when he went. That's where he went to. To the water.

I bet.

Black. Another car.

It's gettin cold eh? Brr. My hands are froze off.

Good thing you're a priest. There's a lot of weirdos out there. Priests are pretty safe eh?

My mother's livin in sin with this guy.

She kicked my father out for nothin.

'Cause she didn't want me to have shit.
'Cause I was shit. Excuse my language.

That's where I'm goin now.
To meet my father at the water.

I haven't been to confession since I was ten.
My mother didn't even care if I went to church.
I only useta go with my father. Daddy'd help me get dressed
up and we'd go Sunday morning and sit right up in the front row
and he'd hold my hand.

I still remember most of the stuff.
I do. Bless me Father... Bless me Father... for I have sinned...
it's been... a million years since my last confession and these are
my sins...
    See.

Do you think God cares? If you do something that you have
to? Like if some people think it's a sin but it isn't? I mean if you
gotta do it?

Like nothing.

Do soldiers go to hell?
For killin people I mean?
That's weird.

He wasn't bad to me you know. Not bad. It was just that...
he stopped pretendin. But he was never bad to me and he never
hit me, well only one time but I hit him first. Sometimes I wanted
him to be bad. Smash me up against the refrigerator so I'd get
knocked out. 'Cause he was doin it on purpose. Sayin he loved
me and that just to make me do it. He made me. Keepin at me all
the time. "C'mere baby, c'mere princess." I wasn't his princess.
He made me you know. Fuck him eh? Just fuck him. FUCK YOU
TIMMY PRINCE. FUCK YOU, YOU SON OF A BITCH!

> *The car stops suddenly. BOB is thrown from her seat into the
> darkness. The car light fades. A new light. BOB is sitting on the
> floor.*

And so. And so. And so. I come home from work and I hate
it. Shampooin hair in some stupid beauty parlour with all these
stupid people and these weirdo guys who give me the creeps. And
Tamara isn't talkin to me for some stupid thing I didn't even do.
Forgettin her birthday or something. How can I FORGET it when
I don't even know when it is. "Well when is it then? When was
it, I never knew when it was, nobody told me." But she won't
say nothin and just keeps on not talkin to me. And I come home.
And there he is. There he is. Sittin on a kitchen chair in the living

room. I hate that so much. Kitchen chairs are for the kitchen. And the TV is on some stupid kind of movie they put on in the afternoon for people who are scared to go outside. And he starts. "C'mere." "C'mere." But ugly. Ugly like he knows I'm not comin here. I'm goin to have a beer 'cause I'm hot but there's none. So I go into the bedroom 'cause I'm gonna listen to some music or somethin but he comes in. He's sayin all this junk but I'm not sayin nothin back 'cause I don't wanna. And he knocks all my stuff on the floor off the dresser. Like that's gonna make me say somethin but it don't. I got nothin to say just "leave me alone" but I'm sick of sayin that. LEAVE ME ALONE. And he goes outta the room. It's quiet. Shh. Quiet. Good. That's good. Quiet. All of a sudden. First real low. He's playin the guitar. So low I'm not sure if I'm really hearin it or if it's just in my head but then he starts singin. Singin... "I brought a love, in a cage, to your house, darling, and I let it go..." Singin that, which I don't want to hear which I really really don't want to hear. Starts singin it louder. I slam the door. More loud then. Loud like I never thought he could sing that loud. Could anyone ever sing that loud? "I brought a love in a cage to your house darling and I let it go... " I got my hands over my ears but I can still hear it. I can still hear it like I'm listenin. But I don't wanna. God! Shit! STOP! STOP! And I get up off the floor 'cause I'm on the floor. I get up off the floor and I go over to the closet. I start pullin stuff out. Diggin through all this stuff. Lookin for it. Lookin. I know it's there. And there it is. The box with the big thick mailman's elastics 'cause the top is broke. I open it up and I'm thinkin about how it was a present from Daddy but he never really gave it to me but it was the one he taught me on and he never took it with him when he left like he wanted me to have it. And there's already bullets in it from long, long ages ago. All I'm thinkin is what if it don't work. What if it don't work? That's in my head but not in my body. My body gets up and walks the long way around through the kitchen to the living room. Not even scared. But my head's freakin out. What if it don't work? What if it don't work? And he's still singin. Loud loud loud and fast. I think I'm cryin. Or my head is. I'm standin right in front of him now. I got it pointed at him. Right at his head. And he knows I'm there and he won't open his eyes and he won't stop singin and he won't stop singin that song... and what if it don't work... and stop. Stop. Stop! Stop! STOP! STOP...

And it worked.

Bang.

Black. Another car. The radio is playing.

Okay if I turn off the radio.
I got this kind of headache.

Thanks.

A lot a' noise in my head.
And can't keep a ride.
Nobody's ever goin farther than a mile east.
Rides and rides and rides.

Shit. It's hard you know. If you ever do it it's hard.

BOB removes her sweater revealing a blood-stained T-shirt.

Look.
My shirt's got all that blood in it.
I can't get it out.
I tried but it wouldn't come.

And you pick him up and...

BOB holds her hands as if cradling a head in her lap.

I was really little and so sick... my mother's goin out some-
where... she comes and sits by me and puts my head in her lap,
my face is pressed right up against her good skirt makin it all wet
with my sweat but she doesn't even care... and she was doin this
to my hair... like this...

Made this neat little hole in the middle of his forehead.
Neat little hole. Then...
Then I see the mess. And in it there's these pieces.
Where the back of his head come off. Three little triangles.
Three of 'em.
I wanna pick them up and see if they fit together.
Like a jigsaw puzzle.
You think they would?

Are we stopping?

Hey! You see that?

That was lilacs.

Right on the side of the highway like that. Nothin else around.

They just grow by themselves you know. Nobody's gotta plant 'em or anything.

Just grow 'cause they want to.

I think... you know... it's good we're stoppin... I think maybe we should go someplace and I should tell somebody about Timmy. 'Cause he's there all by himself... it's so messy... You think? I better eh?

I mean it wasn't like he was so bad or anything.

As the car light fades BOB walks downstage into a new light. BOB is holding the pink dress.

Some day. Some day the little girl grows up. And she is not a princess and she is not a pile of shit. And she buys some of that wallpaper. That wallpaper you see places. And in the catalogue. Where it's a picture? A picture of the woods or a picture of the mountains or a picture of a beach. She gets that wallpaper. The picture of a beach and fills up the whole wall of her bedroom with it. And puts tons of sand all over the floor. This deep with sand. So the room is like a beach. And that's just where she sleeps. No walls no doors no windows. Just beach. And that's where she wakes up. And she would love one day to wake up and walk out into the water right up to her neck.

Imagine what that'd be like eh?

> *We hear* BOB *and Timmy singing Dylan's "I'll Be Your Baby Tonight."* BOB *listens and sways to the music.*

Wild Abandon
A Study of Steve

For V.S.

Wild Abandon was first produced in 1988 by Sword Theatre in association with Theatre Passe Muraille, Toronto.

STEVE   Daniel MacIvor

Directed by Vinetta Strombergs
Designed by Stephan Droege
Slides by Steve Mici Lucas
Stage managed by Chris Humphrey
Original music by Zang Tumb Tumb

The Set

For the Toronto production the set was a black box. The props were a wooden chair, a chain, a white birdcage, and an oversized egg. The back wall was a scrim on which the words and images were projected. While other options are possible, STEVE is a low-tech character most comfortable in low-tech surroundings.

The Images

Slides should be kept to a minimum. Photographic images should be black and white and text should be white typewritten words on a black background. Unless otherwise noted, slide images come up, wait a beat, then black out.

A chair sits centre stage. Lights up on STEVE *standing behind the scrim.*

STEVE

(voice over) "Come into my parlour," said the poet to the chair.

"Can't you see that I'm so lonely and have no one to care? My clothes are all torn and smelling of an unrequited love."

The poet slumped, he rubbed his eyes, he asked the one above:

"Tell the chair to come in here and keep me from myself! My soul has been alone too long upon that dusty shelf."

The chair sat in silence.
The poet was inspired.

Black. Lights up on STEVE *stage left.*

One time? I was a little kid like nine—this woman? We were out in some stupid family rest-o-rant and everybody's fighting in low voices and complaining about the food and that, and this woman, sitting over across at another table, she keeps looking at me, staring at me. I don't say nothing and I start thinking: she's really staring okay! And I start thinking "Hey! This woman, she's my real mother right. She followed me here. She's been watching me for weeks and she's my real mother and she's gonna come over and say 'This boy is my son' and take me away from my stupid ugly family who won't let me do nothing and never let me talk and never let me listen and won't let me have a black room. She'd take me away and out into her new car—that smells new and—a convertible and—with the roof down and we'd drive far away to this house—this castle she lives in and I'd live there too and I'd have my own huge fucking room"...

So I'm thinking this and the woman, she gets up and starts walking over to me. I'm thinking: "HOLY SHIT! HOLY SHIT! It really IS my mother!" I got so nervous. She comes right up to me. Standing right there. I'm sitting down okay, she's right there, and she reaches back... and jabs this fork into my stomach and starts screaming:

DEVIL'S EYES DEVIL'S EYES DEVIL'S EYES!

Pause.

The place went nuts. They had to take me to the hospital... took her away to some rubber room someplace...
Yeah.

That was pretty much the highlight of my life. That and the time Alphonse McKeigan killed the duck in Wentworth Park.

Pause. Sound is of people learning dance steps. Image is of "Dancing." Light on STEVE, *down centre, wrapped in chains.*

There are all different kinds of dancing.

Oh yeah. Tons. Well, four. Yeah. Four.

One. Stage dancing. The kind they do on stage. Ballet or modern or whatever. Chor-e-o-graphed. Someone tells the dancer who went to special schools for years and years where to move and what to feel and they do that. A bunch of people—the ODD-ience—watches. They love it or hate it or don't give a shit. They clap... they applaud.

No matter what they feel, the people watching, they always applaud.

Two. Ballroom dancing. Like waltzing. Two people dance together, touching and that in a certain way. In ballroom dancing they say you don't need an oddience but far as I can see you do. This oddience though they almost never applaud. Except in movies.

Three. Social dancing. This happens at parties sometimes, at wedding receptions and clubs and bars. In this kind there's also couples and it's social because it's not planned out or anything. For fun. Mostly for fun, and for mating purposes. You know, sex.

There's about thirteen, fifteen ways to do this kind of dancing but there's also all this subtle stuff that changes with each person. One time people did certain styles of social dancing. The Mashed Potato. The Cha Cha Cha. The Pony The Hustle The Stroll. Then all these got together with ballroom dancing and turned into disc-O-dancing but that does not exist on the planet anymore.

In social dancing the movements of the dancers is usually pretty uptight because of an unhappy childhood or a very heavy neurosis about death or whatever. Sometimes the movements are free and that but this only happens when the brain gets taken over by some chemical like booze or drugs.

And people watch. But no way, no way do they applaud.

Then there is the best kind of dancing.

Four. This kind doesn't have a name. I could make one up. But I won't. This kind there's no oddience, no steps, no anything, just you. It can happen anytime, anywhere. And the most beautiful... the best music ever is playing. And it's REEEEEALLY LOUD! But it doesn't hurt your ears. But just really like there are about a hundred million speakers all around you and each one plays one note, but perfectly. And everything is... everything.

And the whole world is alive, every tree, every chair, every everything, and you can hear everybody really clapping. And yes. Yes yes yes yes yes... And I am one with the music, I am the music and the dancing and all is one and everything and nothing and I am floating flying flying dancing dancing dancing...

> STEVE raises his arm in the air which pulls the chain tight around his neck, making him gag.

It's very important as one matures to draw a thick dark line between dreams and reality. Four.

Image: "Four." Sound: applause. Black. Lights up on STEVE *facing a white birdcage hanging in the space. In the cage is a large white egg.*

(to egg) There's only one of me. It's just you and me.

And you are mine.

(to audience) Somebody gives you something.

Somebody in your family or somebody you are "with" or somebody you just met or somebody you don't even like but they give you something and even if you don't want it it's yours.

(to egg) Because there's only one of me and they gave you to me so you're mine.

(to audience) And I, me, I can do anything anything anything I want with what's mine. Right?

Pause.

(to egg) See!

(to audience) So, all you got to figure out is what to do with it.

Pause.

After you figure out: what it is.

Black. Music: "Jesus Lifeline." Lights up on STEVE *standing on the chair with a noose around his neck.*

Don't freak out eh. Everybody needs an option.

Screen image:"Op-tion."

OP-TION.

That's a good idea eh? You either do this or you do that. You either have toast or you have cereal. You either get out of bed in the morning or you throw the clock across the room. This is my option. And this here *(stamps chair)* is my step to my option. See? So.

I can either wait around here for something really truly real to happen or… I can climb my stairway to heaven.

I'm full of beauty eh. Metaphors and that. Full of it. Man, I'm so full of beauty I could just… die.

STEVE laughs until he snorts. He snorts until he cries. Black.

Screen image: A window. Lights up. STEVE faces the scrim, his back to the audience. He makes his hands move as the voice of the egg and the sperm, making shadow puppets on the scrim.

The sperm and the egg. The sperm. And. The egg.
The sperm and the egg.
"Stevie."
The sperm and the egg.
"Stevie!"

The sperm——

"STEVIE!"

What?

"Here's your rosary."

I don't need it.

"You take your beads!

Have you got your ticket Stevie?"

Yeah.

"And here I made you some bologna sandwiches for the plane. And don't you go hungry for pride! And here, your long underwear."

Ma!

"Stevie, just because you're leaving home doesn't mean you're not going to get cold anymore. And take these."

What are they?

"Just take them. Put one in each pocket."

What for?

"STEVIE JUST DO AS I SAY!"

STEVE turns and addresses the audience.

Little pieces of paper and on each one she had all filled out: my name, my address, my phone number, and I AM A CATHOLIC PLEASE CALL A PRIEST.

STEVE turns back.

Ma I told you a hundred times I'm not a Catholic anymore!

"STEVIE! You were born a Catholic of two Catholics you were christened a Catholic confirmed a Catholic you went to Catholic school and you will be a Catholic for all eternity whether you like it or not!"

Pause.

Why one in every pocket?

"Because. In case the plane was to crash and you were to get all burned up or split apart there'd be a better chance they'd find one."

The egg. And. Theeeeeee Sperm! *(bringing up the other hand)*

Bye Da.

"Stevie?"

What?

"Uh. You uh. You. Watch yourself."

Okay.

"Stevie…"

Yeah?

"You… Listen to me now."

What?

"Just. Don't go getting in any trouble."

I won't.

"But just…"

What!

"You just keep your pecker in your pants until you find a girl you want to marry!"

The image of the window disappears. STEVE *steps up into the shaft of light.*

Doesn't every kid want to have a black room? An all-black room? I did? All black. The walls black, the floor black, and black curtains on the window so only one little stream of light comes through and in it you see all the dust and shit in the air. Yeah! They wouldn't let me though. Most kids don't get their black room they got to spend their whole life looking for it.

The sperm and the egg.

The sperm and the egg.

The sperm and the egg.

The sperm and the egg!

If my sperm had ever hit an egg, I would've let the kid have its black room right away and got it over with.

Black. Sound: whistling. Lights up. STEVE *is whistling into the cage.*

I had a cat once. It didn't have a name. People think that's weird eh. Not naming a cat. But you know what? I don't think they want names. And when me and the cat were alone in the house? I'd do this... I'd do this certain series of... acts to it.

Interest piqued?

First. I'd throw him across the bedroom ten or twelve times. Not into a wall or anything, just onto the bed. Second, I'd grab his front paws in one hand, his back paws in the other hand and swing him around for thirteen–fifteen seconds. Then, I'd take the lid off the garbage can, put him in the garbage can, put the lid on the garbage can, and bang on the sides: bangbangbangbangbang-bangbangbangbangbang real fast for, I don't know, ten seconds.

Then! Oh man!

Then I'd take the lid off the can and STAND BACK!

That cat would fly!

FLY! And then disappear for like an hour, maybe more.

But. I didn't LIKE doing that to him. I didn't do that to him because I liked it. It was to see him fly. And! And the real reason why I did it was to help him realize how lucky he was to have his freedom.

Pause.

But you know what? You could tell that, like after a while, after he got over it and that, like a day or something later, you could tell by the way he stretched into the sunlight on the living-room carpet, you could tell, he didn't remember a goddamn thing about it. Fucking cats eh?

Pause.

I'm glad I told you that.

> *Black. Screen image: "possi." Lights up. STEVE is opening the cage.*
> *Screen image: "bili." Throughout the following STEVE takes the*
> *egg from the cage and holds it up to the light.*

It might be. It might be. It might be. It might be. It might be. It might be. It might be.

> *STEVE replaces the egg and closes the cage door.*

It might be.

> *Lights fade. Screen image: "ties." Music: loud rock. STEVE is strad-*
> *dling the chair, laughing.*

This buddy of mine? This old buddy of mine. Crab. Crab, that was his name. Good guy excellent guy. Haven't seen him in... Big tall guy. And he had these hands right? Both his hands. Each one had a thumb, like a normal thumb, but his four fingers, these four fingers on both hands were all mushed up together, all joined together like one great big finger. Shit he was a funny guy. And we'd go out right, like to meet people at some bar or something and say like there'd be these people he never met before? He'd come in, sit down, be like: "Hi" like: yeah right whatever; then, after a couple of minutes, he'd take his hands and put them up flat on the table like this. Right okay? Like this. Then, all of a sudden, like one by one maybe, everybody'd notice. And it would get reeeeeally quiet. Quiet but like loud so you're deaf from it. Nobody could talk and I'm trying not to break up 'cause I know what's coming. Then, sure as shit man sure as shit some dick'd go: "Um, what did you say your name was?"

And he'd go: *(waving his hands in the air like claws)*

"Crab!" Oh man it was beautiful. Crab? Get it get it!

Oh man. They'd freak out. Shit.

And you know what?

Nobody'd mention his hands. NOBODY'D MENTION HIS FUCK-ING HANDS!

And you know what else? Crab didn't give a sweet shit.

ALL RIGHT BUDDY! Man, Crab could handle anything. Made me wish I was born without a nose or something.

     STEVE covers his nose with one hand and extends the other.

Hi there.

Beak.

     Black. STEVE sits up centre in the chair.

Shit.

Screen image:"shit."

Shit man shit. Shit shit shit.

Everything is shit. Everywhere is shit. Everywhere you read, you turn on the TV, the radio: Shit! Buy this do that be this.

Shit!

People. People you talk to.

People sticking their holes right up against your ear and taking a big long shit into your brain. Then you come home what do you have to do? You have to shit!

Shit!

But that doesn't do nothing. You can shit your head off but you're still full of it.

Every teeny tiny little cell man. And you can poke and pull and squeeeeeeeeeze... But man, there's no way you can get it all out. No way. Still there. Oh! But... Shit's good right? Yeah. It's good.

'Cause: everybody's got it and everybody does it and it's what keeps us all humble and makes us all the same.

So that's what it is.

Pause.

WELL THAT'S FUCKING ENCOURAGING!

Black. Sound: a crowded bar that fades throughout next scene. Lights up. STEVE is standing with a chair.

Okay. You're out in some bar or something and you're talking to someone or yourself... or someone say, and you're just talking and that and doing what you do when you talk that you don't even know that you do but you do that you don't even think about but you do. Making faces. Weird faces.

Sitting funny with your head stuck out say. And you've got your arms like this say and you're going like this. You're telling a story about how you came this close to winning something. Money say.

Or how you got fired for telling your boss to take his job and shove it and his whole goddamn family especially his ugly daughter... And you notice this jerk... Over on the other side of the bar. You can just see him out of the corner of your eye but you can tell the guy's a jerk. So you just think: "Jerk" and keep going.

Then it's getting weird: This jerk is sort of looking at you it looks like.

"What's that jerk looking at?" So... you stop telling your story. And you're all ready to look at this jerk and make this face of: "What's your problem?" or whatever.

STEVE turns to face the jerk.

It's a mirror.

Black. Lights up. Steve is cutting diagonally across from the cage.

Hey!

Hey hey hey hey!
Hey! You!
Come here.
You! Hey! Come here!
What are you waiting for?
What are you waiting for?

    STEVE approaches the egg.

What are you waiting for, I'm asking you what you are waiting for! Don't you know it's rude not to answer a person's question? Didn't your mother ever teach you—

    Pause.

Yeah yeah sorry sorry.

    STEVE sits on the floor facing the egg.

You don't smoke do you?

    Black. Sound: a rattlesnake. STEVE approaches the cage singing.

"L is for the way you Look at me. O is for the only One I see. V is Very very extraordinary. E is Even more than…"

Funny about that eh?

You make this friend. You make this friend at a party or the laund-ro-mat. You make this friend. You like this person. You spend time with this person. A lot of time. You tell this person here things about yourself, your family. Secret things. Things you always thought were secrets. This person sees you naked. In the daytime. You put your mouth on this person. On their body. Places you never thought you'd touch with your mouth. But you do. And you like it. Because. This person is your friend.

Because you...

Oh yeah.

Oh yeah oh yeah oh baby oh yeah yes yeah yes do that yes do that yes oh yeah oh baby oh baby oh baby...

A scream begins. No sound.

There it is!

People scream eh?

They're supposed to.

Even if you're by yourself you should scream because... it's scary! Never worry about screaming. Shake the walls, crack the ceiling, let the curtain in the temple be rent in two... oh yeah. What you got to worry about is if there's no scream. Man if somebody doesn't scream then you better get help. Because everybody should scream when they come.

You know why they call it come?

They call it come because you come... this close... to nothing. That's where it is, where everything is nothing and you are not and the whole world is like this big huge lung so full it's about to explode but this big huge lung full of... nothing. Zero. That close to zero. They call it the big "O" but it's not enough, not "OH," it's ZERO. Being zero. Nothing. No things. No thoughts. No feelings. Only...

Doesn't it just make you want to scream though?

Oh yeah.

Oh yeah oh yeah oh baby oh yeah yes yeah yes do that yes do that yes oh yeah oh baby oh baby oh baby... I LOVE YOU!!!

Ooops.

Looooovvvvvve. It doesn't exist really. That kind of L-O-V-E, Nat King Cole kind of love does not.

Well it does. For virgins... and pop singers... and poets.

That love is actually just fear wearing nice perfume.

That's what someone once told me. Fear.

"The terror of knowing that you have put yourself in a position where another human being has control over you and might, and probably will, do everything they can to destroy you." TO DESTROY YOU!

Love is fear in a nice neighbourhood.

And there's a lot of energy out there calling itself love and you never know when you might turn a corner and...

BLAM! find yourself inside it.

So you have to be careful.

I'm not bitter or anything.

Love does not exist.

Love is lust. Fear. Yeah.

Pause.

(to audience) BOO!

STEVE laughs. Pause.

(to egg) Boo.

Screen image: "boo." Black. Lights up. STEVE is in the chair leaning against the stage left wall.

I go to this diner.

Not a rest-o-rant I hate rest-o-rants I never go to rest-o-rants I only go to diners. And I only go to diners that have all-day breakfasts because who the hell are they to tell me when I should eat breakfast? Who the hell are they to tell me when I should get out of bed? This particular breakfast this particular day was three, four o'clock. Sausages, hash browns, WHITE toast, BLACK coffee, and eggs over EASY. Very easy, so you can still almost... taste... that... chicken.

Sometimes jam sometimes not depends on the day this day no. So I'm sitting there looking out the window thinking about how when trees are dead and the leaves are gone you can see so much more of the world and this woman four, four and a half feet away left side starts talking to her friend in this pretty loud voice about this trip she took to Mexico.

"There were so many gringos."

Yeah. I'm serious. Gringos. That's what she said.

And then? Every time the guy brings something over to the table she goes, "Gracias!"

Gracias like she took one trip there and she turns into fucking Mexico. But that be okay, but that be okay until she starts talking about being on this bus with all these "men" and she says "men" like it's some kind of disease or a new drug. "Men."

And what am I? I'm a man. I'm a man sitting right there. She'd be looking right at me if she'd just turn her head this much. She practically is staring at me without even moving her eyes at all. I'm right there!

Then! Out of nowhere, she's telling her friend about the Grand Canyon. The fucking Grand Canyon's not in Mexico!

What am I supposed to think right?

THEN! Fuck... Then she's describing this dream she had where all these "men" are growing out of the walls in her apartment. All these "men." So I was pretty fed up right—

And not because she's a woman, don't think that okay, I got nothing against women—

Fake mothers I do! Fake mothers who come up to you in rest-o-rants and stab you in the guts with a fork I do! But this woman here it was just her Person-Ality that was pissing me off... and how she was saying all this shit just so somebody would hear her. I'm sitting right there!

So.

So I lean over and I say: "Excuse me. Why don't you go get some help!" Yeah I did.

No I didn't.

I didn't say that.

What I said was, "If you want to sleep with me why don't you just say so?"

No I didn't.

I didn't say nothing.

Crab would've though. First though he would've waved his hands around a bit.

Pause.

But you know what I did do though?

I got up, and I changed my seat!

That's almost as good as saying something.

And I never went back to that diner either.

Not because of her… but because they got my fucking eggs wrong!

Black. Sound: a cuckoo clock strikes three. Screen image: "False Mother #2." Lights up. STEVE centre stage.

Beware the cuckoo!

Oh yeah, everybody thinks they're so great. Those wooden clocks and that. HA! I can just see those little cuckoo bastards rubbing their little wings together and laughing over that one.

The female cuckoo, when she's going to have a baby, finds another kind of bird's nest with new-laid eggs in it and lays her egg there. Her ONE egg. And then she just takes off to fuck knows where. The other bird comes home and figures she just counted wrong or something and starts hatching it with the other eggs... So anyway... the cuckoo egg hatches first, the mother bird just thinks it's a preemie or something and goes out looking for food for it. And then, fuck, this little cuckoo bastard pushes all the other eggs out of the nest, the real children, so it can have all the food for itself. The fake mother bird? She goes for it. Just a run of bad luck she thinks.

Now.

You might think that this fake mother bird is stupid or something for letting herself be duped like that but NO! See it's trust. Blind trust man. This is her kid we're talking about here, she thinks it's her kid. She fucking loves this egg. Fuck.

So anyway, this fake mother bird feeds this jerk-off cuckoo. Feeds it and feeds it and feeds it until it's big enough to fly away... and then it just fucking takes off... nothing, not a howd'ya do, nothing. Gone.

It's wild. Fucking abandonment man. Abandonment. Big stuff. Really big stuff. Like you know? Big time. Fuck man, the cuckoo's got no heart.

The cuckoo's got no fucking heart!

Black. Lights up. STEVE *is squatting centre stage.*

I am a unique person.

I am special.

I am a unique and special one-of-a-kind person.

I am not like anyone else.

I am myself and that is like nothing else in this or any other world.

Pause.

This is Earth right? We're on Earth. And we know these planets: Mercury, Venus, Earth, Mars, Jupiter, Saturn, Uranus, Neptune, Pluto. And they all move around the sun. At the middle. But all these planets go around the sun and the same time they're spinning around themselves in tiny little circles. Going around and spinning at the same time. AND each, or most, of these planets have moons. Little planets that go around these other first planets. Earth's just got one moon but some planets have more, one planet's got like SEVEN or something! So. Going around and spinning and going around all this frigging moving okay? And we're on Earth. And we're all moving around stuff all the time, even when we sleep. And there are, I don't know, billions of people on Earth, zillions, trillions, whatever that is but it's like more than anybody could ever count in like a hundred lifetimes or whatever.

BUT!

I am a unique person. I am special. I am a unique and special one-of-a-kind person. I am not like anyone else. I am myself and that is like nothing else in this or any other world.

Fuck!

Pause.

Fuuuuuuuck.

Black. Lights up. STEVE *is bouncing off the walls in the space.*

Like... like... like... like like like. Walking around walking around walking around or in a room full of people a box full of people arms legs eyes feet faces stuff and BRAINS! BRAINS! BRAINS! In every person is a brain! ALL these brains in shells all over the place.

Think now.

Pause.

See!

That was your brain working that was your BRAIN!

That's where all the action is. Inside's where. So how come I can't see the action? How come! *(noticing egg)*

Maybe... Maybe it might be that. Okay.

Say. Say. Say this here egg here. All you see is the shell, but that's nothing, all the real stuff, all the live stuff, that's inside.

I could... break it open. I could. Then I'd see it.
But then it'd be dead.
I could cook it and eat it.
But then it be shit.
No.
Just like this here.
This is how it's an egg.
You just gotta wait.
All right then.
I'll wait.

Pause.

Man oh man I would really really really like to have a little chat with God.

Black. Sound: rattling of a chain. Lights up on STEVE *counting the links of a chain.*

The chain man. Chain. The chain. See, the whole frigging world is all wrapped up in this great big chain. The whole frigging world. And this chain, it's made up of these things. These things: You're born. You work. You die. You're born you work you die you're born you work you die you're born you work you die you're born you work and like that. And inside that there's all this other stuff. Stuff. You eat you sleep you shit you breathe you eat you sleep you shit you breathe you eat you sleep you shit you. Okay? But it's all this big chain around everything. Now. You take one of those things, say you take "you breathe" you take "you breathe" and you say "I am not going to do that anymore." So you don't. You stop breathing. You hold your breath.

Pause.

Then, either you change your mind and start breathing again or... you kick off. And even if you do kick off you're lucky if maybe two maybe ONE person is even fucked up about it for like a year right? And that's lucky. Because? Life goes on, right? Life goes on. It doesn't go over or up or down or whatever. It doesn't go BUUUUUUUZZZZZZZZZ, it doesn't go VAAAAAAAAAAAARRRRRRRR-ROOOOOOOOOOMMMMMM, or like that. It goes... ON. Life goes on.

STEVE approaches the cage and spins it violently.

On and on and on and on and on and on and on and on and on and on and on and on. Because everybody's everybody's everybody's!...
All right.
All right.
I'm coming home.

STEVE places the chair downstage centre.

I'm coming home.

I'm coming home and I'm walking up the sidewalk I'm walking up the sidewalk and there's my house and I see my house and I get to my house and I turn to walk up the steps—

And there's this guy on the lawn. Laying on the lawn. The front lawn where I live. I think: Oh so he's passed out, but no, his eyes are open. So, he's having a little rest. I go on my way. Then I hear him, breathing. He's really stiff right and he's breathing like this. Through his teeth. Like he's running really fast. But he's not. He's really still right. And I think: Maybe I should go over and ask this guy is he okay and then I think what a stupid fucking question that would be 'cause look at the guy he's not okay. So I'm just gonna go in. Then he's talking. But not to me. He's looking up at the sky and talking through his teeth saying: COME ON COME ON COME ON COME ON COME ON COME ON COME ON COME ON.

I stop for a second. Then I go in the house.

And I go upstairs and I stand in the front window and I watch this guy.

I can't hear him but I can see he's still breathing through his teeth and going: COME ON COME ON COME ON COME ON COME ON.

I watch this guy, all day, and I ask myself...

What. Is. He. Waiting. For.

What?

WHAT THE FUCK IS HE WAITING FOR? What am I waiting for? What's everybody waiting for? Everybody's waiting. Everybody's waiting for something.

(to egg) You hear me? You hear me? What am I waiting for? What? For some life to start? For some woman who I think is my

mother to come up and stab me in the guts with a fork? For some life to end? What!

Well I'm sick! You hear me? I'm sick. I'm sick of waiting.

And I'm through waiting for YOU!

> STEVE *strikes the birdcage with the chair. Black. Sound: crushing metal, shattering glass, a flock of birds, a high C, a siren. Lights up.* STEVE *is sitting on the chair, centre stage. He is panting.*

The day Alphonse McKeigan killed the duck in Wentworth Park I was there. Alphonse and the boys were over across the pond and I was sitting on this side watching them. I had a book. I was pretending to read a book. I used to do that when I was a kid, pretend to be reading a book so I could watch things. They were smoking cigarettes and laughing. Then they go around to behind the bandshell where the pond gets smaller. After a few minutes I hear all this yelling and splashing and that and I figure Alphonse threw in his brother Victor or some other of those assholes so I go around to see. I get there they're all throwing rocks into the middle. I don't know what they're throwing at. I don't see nothing.

Then I see it.

This duck.

They're just missing it.

And then this duck, it swims right for me. Right at me. I'm almost getting hit by these rocks now and this duck it comes right up by me. Trying to get up the bank, and it does, the boys come tearing across the pond after it like they were walking on water.

Chasing this duck. And they get it, caught up by the fence. The boys fall back and it's just Alphonse and the duck. He's going at it with these rocks, I don't know where they're coming from. WAP WAP, picking up rocks that already hit it and giving it to him again, WAP WAP. And I'm thinking: I should do something or even just yell or something. But I don't, first I think it's 'cause I'm scared but I'm not. It's 'cause I want to watch. This guy is killing something. Killing something!

I never seen anything get killed before. That must be... that must be the most power in the whole world. The most power in the whole world.

The noose is flown in. STEVE fixates on it. Sound: elongated birdcage smash, siren, etc.

There's only one of me. There's only one of me. There's only one of me. There's only one of me. There's only one of me. ONE. There's only one of me. There's only one of me. There's only one of me. There's only one of me. TWO. There's only one of me. There's only one of me. There's only one of me. There's only one of me. There's only one of me. THREE.

Silence.

There's only one of me.
There is only one of me.
Four.

STEVE knocks the chair over.

Dance dance dance dance dance dance dance dance!

Black.

The end.

author photo by Guntar Kravis

Daniel MacIvor is one of Canada's most accomplished playwrights and performers. Winner of the prestigious Elinore and Lou Siminovitch Prize, the GLAAD Award, the Governor General's Literary Award, and many others, Daniel's plays have been met with acclaim throughout North America.